Harp Seals

by Kathleen Martin-James

Lerner Publications Company • Minneapolis

For Kate

I am grateful for the help of seal experts Dr. W. Don Bowen and Blair Fricker. Thanks, as always, to Dr. Mike James for his patience and cheerfulness in answering many scientific questions relating to this book.

The images in this book are used with the permission of: © blickwinkel/Alamy, p. 4; © Laura Westlund/Independent Picture Service, pp. 4-5; © Aflo/naturepl.com, p. 6; AP Photo/Jonathan Hayward, pp. 7, 11, 37, 39, 42, 47; © Fred Bruemmer/Peter Arnold, Inc., pp. 8, 22, 32; © Brian J. Skerry/National Geographic/Getty Images, pp. 9, 19, 24, 25, 34, 40, 43; © Jeff Foott/Discovery Channel Images/Getty Images, pp. 10, 26, 33; © Michio Hoshino/Minden Pictures, p. 12; © Gerald & Buff Corsi/Visuals Unlimited, p. 13; © Doug Allan/naturepl.com, pp. 14, 29, 36; © Bruce Coleman Brakefield/Alamy, p. 15; © age fotostock/SuperStock, p. 16; © Stephen J. Krassmann/Photo Researchers, Inc., p. 17; © Stone Nature Photography/Alamy, p. 18; © Kevin Schafer/CORBIS, p. 20; © Flip Nicklin/Minden Pictures/Getty Images, p. 21; © Harald Sund/Photographer's Choice/Getty Images, p. 23; © Daisy Gilardini/The Image Bank/Getty Images, p. 27; © Dan Guravich/CORBIS, p. 28; © Photodisc/Getty Images, p. 30; © Johnny Johnson/Stone/Getty Images, p. 31; © Joe McDonald/Visuals Unlimited, p. 35; © Patricio Robles Gil/Sierra Madre/Minden Pictures/Getty Images, p. 38; © Richard Olsenius/ National Geographic/Getty Images, p. 41; © Klein/Peter Arnold, Inc., p. 46; © Daniel J. Cox/ Riser/Getty Images, p. 48 (top); © Natural Visions/Alamy, p. 48 (bottom).

Front Cover: © Kevin Schafer/Stone/Getty Images.

Lerner Publications Company
A division of Lerner Publishing Group, Inc.
241 First Avenue North
Minneapolis, MN 55401 U.S.A.

Website address: www.lernerbooks.com

Library of Congress Cataloging-in-Publication Data

Martin-James, Kathleen.
    Harp seals / by Kathleen Martin-James.
        p. cm. — (Early bird nature books)
    Includes index.
        ISBN: 978–0–8225–7889–5 (lib. bdg. : alk. paper)
        1. Harp seal—Juvenile literature. I. Title.
    QL737.P64M355 2009
    599.79'29—dc22   2007042169

Manufactured in the United States of America
1 2 3 4 5 6 – BP – 14 13 12 11 10 09

Contents

GREENLAND

CANADA

NORWAY

NORTH
AMERICA

NORTH
ATLANTIC
OCEAN

EUROPE

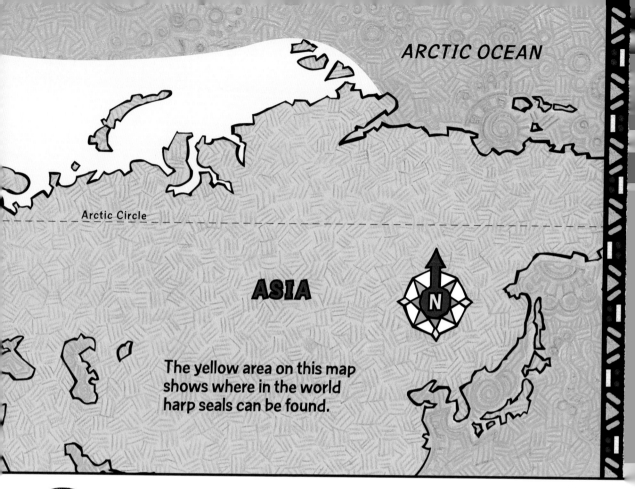

ARCTIC OCEAN

Arctic Circle

ASIA

N

The yellow area on this map
shows where in the world
harp seals can be found.

Be a Word Detective

*Can you find these words as you read about the harp seal's
life? Be a detective and try to figure out what they mean.
You can turn to the glossary on page 46 for help.*

blubber
climate
cow
habitat

**marine
  mammals**
migrate
molting
nurse

pack ice
pelt
predators
prey
pups

Chapter 1

This harp seal is resting on ice. Where did its name come from?

Lover of Ice

The harp seal is named after a musical instrument called a harp. That may seem a little strange. But take a close look at an adult harp seal. Can you see the black marks on its back?

A harp has a curvy triangle shape. Long ago, someone thought the shape on this kind of seal's back looked like a harp.

The black harp markings are a little bit different on each harp seal.

Harp seals have other names too. Some people call them saddleback seals. Other people call them Greenland seals. The name that scientists gave harp seals might describe them best of all. In English, it means "lover of ice."

The name scientists give harp seals is Pagophilus groenlandicus.

When harp seals swim quickly, they hold their front flippers against the sides of their bodies. Then they use their rear flippers to push themselves through the water.

Ice is very important to harp seals. They spend most of their time swimming near ice or resting on it.

This harp seal is poking its head through a hole in the ice. Harp seals have large eyes. This helps them to see underwater.

On the ice, adult harp seals are easy to spot. This is because of the black marks on their backs. Harp seals also have black faces with whiskers. The rest of their fur is silver.

Like all seals, harp seals have long, round bodies. Adult harp seals are almost 6 feet long. That is about as long as a bed. They usually weigh about 285 pounds.

Harp seals often stretch their back flippers straight out behind them when they are on the ice.

A harp seal's claws are at the end of its flippers. Its claws are dark, just like the markings on its back.

Harp seals have four flippers. The two short flippers in front have strong claws. The two back flippers are long and thin. Harp seals use their flippers to swim in the ocean. They also use their front flippers and claws to pull themselves across the ice.

Harp seals are marine (muh-REEN) mammals. Marine mammals are mammals that spend time in the ocean. They are excellent swimmers. But they cannot breathe underwater. Marine mammals must come to the water's surface for air. Whales, dolphins, sea otters, and polar bears are also marine mammals.

Sea otters, like harp seals, are marine mammals. Sea otters spend a lot of time floating on their backs in the icy water.

Chapter 2

This harp seal is underwater. What is it swimming near?

Living in Icy Water

The place where an animal lives is called its habitat (HAB-uh-tat). Harp seals live in the Arctic Ocean and the North Atlantic Ocean. The water in these oceans is so cold that many animals cannot live in it. It is so cold that it has pack ice floating in it. Pack ice is frozen seawater. Harp seals usually stay close to pack ice.

This harp seal looks down through a hole in the pack ice.

Harp seals need blubber to stay warm in their cold habitat. Blubber is a thick layer of fat underneath the seal's skin. An adult harp seal's blubber is usually about 4 inches thick.

Even though it is covered in snow, this harp seal stays warm.

A harp seal's fur also helps to keep it warm in its cold habitat.

The blubber keeps the seal warm in the same way that a snowsuit helps keep you warm.

Blubber also helps a seal float in the water. Seals do not have blubber on their flippers.

Blubber is important for other reasons too. Blubber gives the harp seal its smooth shape. A smooth body helps harp seals swim easily and quickly through the water. Blubber also stores energy from the food harp seals eat.

Harp seals use energy to help them do things like swim and hunt.

This harp seal dives into the water from the pack ice above.

This harp seal is searching for food.

Harp seals hunt for food underwater. They search under pack ice, and they dive deep in the water. Harp seals do not hunt for only one kind of food. They try many things. They grab their prey (PRAY) with their teeth. They swallow their food whole or in big chunks. They spit out the food they don't want.

Harp seals eat fish called Arctic cod, polar cod, Atlantic herring, and capelin (KAP-eh-lihn) most often. Harp seals also eat animals called crustaceans (cruh-STAY-shuns). Crustaceans live in the sea and have a hard shell. Crab, lobster, and shrimp are crustaceans.

These young fish are called polar cod. They are hiding in the cracks in the ice.

Chapter 3

This harp seal pops its head up through a small hole in the ice. What is it doing?

Following the Open Water

Harp seals often swim under the pack ice. When they need to breathe, they find a hole in the ice. They poke their heads up through the hole for air. Harp seals will drown if they cannot find air to breathe. So they need to be near open water. Open water is water that is not covered by ice.

It gets colder in the Arctic Ocean in wintertime. More pack ice fills the water. There are so many pieces of ice that they crash into one another. They join to form huge, bumpy ice fields. Then there is very little open water.

This is a field of pack ice.

As it gets colder, harp seals must swim south to find more open water. It is warmer in the south. There is less ice. The seals migrate (MY-grayt) just before winter comes. *Migrate* means "to move from one place to another at around the same time each year." Seals do not migrate with their family. They travel alone.

This harp seal is swimming off the east coast of Canada. Pack ice floats beside the seal. Open water is above it.

These harp seals are lying together on a field of pack ice. Open water is at the edges of the pack ice.

But they will often meet up with other seals that are also migrating.

Harp seals swim a very long way to get to their winter habitat. Some migrate to the northwest coast of Russia. Some swim to pack ice near the east coast of Greenland. Most harp seals migrate to the east coast of Canada.

This harp seal is in its winter habitat.

Harp seals will stay in their winter habitat until spring. In the spring, the ocean water gets warmer. The pack ice melts. Then the harp seals migrate back north to the Arctic Ocean.

The ice fields in the Arctic Ocean do not melt. But in the spring, the water there warms up. This makes the huge ice fields break apart into smaller pieces of pack ice. Enough ice and open water are around for the harp seals to live there again.

This pack ice is beginning to melt.

Chapter 4

The small white seal in this picture is a baby. What do we call a baby seal?

Growing Up

Mother seals give birth on the pack ice when they are in their winter habitat. Mother seals are called cows. Baby seals are called pups.

All harp seal cows have their pups at about

the same time. Pups are always born at the end of February or the beginning of March. At that time of year, hundreds of cows climb onto the pack ice together. Father seals stay in the water and will not meet their pups.

This is a group of male seals swimming near the pack ice. Male seals are called bulls.

A cow will usually have one pup each year. When a pup is born, it does not look like an adult harp seal. It has white, fluffy fur on its body. It does not have a black harp mark on its back.

A pup's white fur blends with the snow. This helps to keep it safe from other animals that might want to eat it.

A young pup does not have a lot of blubber. Lying under the sun helps to keep it warm.

Newborn pups are about 33 inches long. They weigh about 24 pounds. That is about the size of a two-year-old child. New pups do not have much blubber in their bodies. But they will need blubber to keep them warm on the ice.

This pup is nursing on the pack ice.

Pups grow bigger and add more blubber
by eating. Pups nurse, like all mammals. That
means they drink milk from their mother's
body. It is their first food.

The cow stays near her pup after it is born.
After two days, she leaves it on the ice while

she swims. She will come back to nurse her pup. There are many pups on the ice at the same time. The cow knows her pup by how it looks, smells, and sounds.

This cow sniffs the pup to make sure it is hers. This is called a harp seal "kiss."

This pup has fallen into the water by mistake. Its mother helps to push it back up onto the ice.

The pup grows very quickly. After 12 days, the pup weighs about 79 pounds. That is about as much as an 11-year-old child weighs. The cow leaves her pup and does not come back. The pup cries for its mother. But soon it learns to live by itself. After a few weeks, it can swim in the water. Then the pup finds fish and small crustaceans to eat.

This pup is crying out for its mother.

When a harp seal is about two weeks old, it will begin to lose its white fur and grow new fur. This is called molting. The new fur is gray with black spots. The harp seal will molt again when it is about 13 months old.

The white fur on this pup has started to fall out.

When harp seal pups have lost all of their white fur, they are called beaters.

After that, a harp seal molts every year. But it will not change how it looks every year. Some harp seals will always be gray with black spots. They will never have a harp pattern on their fur. But most harp seals will have the black harp pattern. This will happen by the time they are five years old.

Chapter 5

A polar bear drags a harp seal it killed across the ice. What other animals eat harp seals?

Harp Seal Predators

Like most animals, harp seals have predators (PREH-duh-turz). Predators are animals that hunt and eat other animals. Polar bears, killer whales, and sharks are all predators of harp seals.

Harp seals are also hunted by people. People hunt harp seals for food. They also hunt harp seals for the oil in their skin. People use harp seal oil in oil lamps and for cooking.

This is a sealing boat. It carries seal hunters to the pack ice where the harp seals are. Seal hunters are often called sealers.

People use the harp seal's pelt too. The pelt is the skin and fur of the seal. People make clothing out of harp seal pelts.

This sealer loads pelts onto the sealing boat.

Someday, there may be other problems for harp seals. Scientists think climate (KLY-muht) change may cause trouble for the seals. Climate is what the weather of a place is usually like. If the climate where seals live gets too warm, less pack ice will form. Then there may not be enough places for harp seals to give birth to their pups and nurse them. This means not as many pups would live to be adults.

Smaller chunks of pack ice are called ice floes. In this picture, ice floes float near the edge of a field of pack ice.

But these "lovers of ice" are safe for now. Harp seals can be found swimming, diving, and hunting near pack ice in their ocean habitat.

These harp seals are resting on the ice in the sunshine.

This pup swims by itself for the first time. Its mother watches nearby.

A NOTE TO ADULTS
ON SHARING A BOOK

When you share a book with a child, you show that reading is important. To get the most out of the experience, read in a comfortable, quiet place. Turn off the television and limit other distractions, such as telephone calls.

Be prepared to start slowly. Take turns reading parts of this book. Stop occasionally and discuss what you're reading. Talk about the photographs. If the child begins to lose interest, stop reading. When you pick up the book again, revisit the parts you have already read.

BE A VOCABULARY DETECTIVE

The word list on page 5 contains words that are important in understanding the topic of this book. Be word detectives and search for the words as you read the book together. Talk about what the words mean and how they are used in the sentence. Do any of these words have more than one meaning? You will find the words defined in a glossary on page 46.

WHAT ABOUT QUESTIONS?

Use questions to make sure the child understands the information in this book. Here are some suggestions:

What did this paragraph tell us? What does this picture show? What group of animals do harp seals belong in? What do harp seals eat? Who are the harp seal's predators? How do harp seals breathe? What is your favorite part of the book? Why?

If the child has questions, don't hesitate to respond with questions of your own, such as What do *you* think? Why? What is it that you don't know? If the child can't remember certain facts, turn to the index.

INTRODUCING THE INDEX

The index helps readers find information without searching through the whole book. Turn to the index on page 48. Choose an entry such as *claws*, and ask the child to use the index to find out what harp seals use their claws for. Repeat this exercise with as many entries as you like. Ask the child to point out the differences between an index and a glossary. (The index helps readers find information, while the glossary tells readers what words mean.)

LEARN MORE ABOUT
HARP SEALS

BOOKS

Aloian, Molly, and Bobbie Kalman. *The Arctic Habitat.* Saint Catharines, ONT.: Crabtree Publishing, 2007. Learn about the plants and animals that live in the harp seal's arctic habitat. The book's design makes the information easy to find and fun to read.

Ganeri, Anita. *I Wonder Why the Sea Is Salty? and Other Questions about the Oceans.* Boston: Kingfisher, 2003. This question-and-answer book tells all about oceans, including facts about how big and deep the ocean is and how waves form.

Hodge, Deborah. *Who Lives Here? Polar Animals.* Toronto: Kids Can Press, 2008. Get to know more about seals and the other animals that live in the coldest parts of our world. This simple picture book gives basic facts about polar animals.

Woodward, John. *Oceans Atlas: An Amazing Aquatic Adventure.* New York: Dorling Kindersley, 2007. Dive into the oceans of the world with this atlas. It is full of information about the sea and the animals living in it. It has photos, maps, and a CD-ROM.

WEBSITES

Brian Skerry Photography
http://brianskerry.com/portfolio.html
Travel with National Geographic photographer Brian Skerry as he explores the arctic. The wonderful photographs and story will help you imagine the world of the harp seal.

Harp Seals
http://www.enchantedlearning.com/subjects/mammals/pinniped/Harpsealprintout.shtml
This site has facts about harp seals and a diagram of a harp seal.

Harp Seals
http://www.nature.ca/notebooks/English/harpseal.htm
This online animal dictionary includes many important harp seal facts and information on lots of other wildlife.

GLOSSARY

blubber: the thick layer of fat underneath the skin of harp seals. Blubber stores energy and helps to keep harp seals warm.

climate (KLY-muht): the usual weather of a place

cows: adult female harp seals

habitat (HAB-uh-tat): the place where an animal lives

mammals: animals that breathe air, have hair, and drink their mothers' milk

marine (muh-REEN) mammals: animals with backbones and hair that live in the ocean but breathe air

migrate (MY-grayt): to move from one place to another when seasons change

molting: when animals lose their fur so that new fur can grow

nurse: to drink milk from a mother's body

pack ice: frozen seawater

pelt: a harp seal's skin and fur

predators (PREH-duh-turz): animals that hunt and eat other animals

prey (PRAY): animals that are hunted and eaten by other animals

pups: baby harp seals

INDEX

Pages listed in **bold** type refer to photographs.